COOL CAREERS WITHOUT COLLEGE FOR
PEOPLE
WHO LOVE
TO TRAVEL

COOL CAREERS WITHOUT COLLEGE FOR PEOPLE WHO LOVE TO TRAVEL

SIMONE PAYMENT

The Rosen Publishing Group, Inc.

New York

Published in 2004 by The Rosen Publishing Group, Inc.
29 East 21st Street, New York, NY 10010

Library of Congress Cataloging-in-Publication Data

Payment, Simone.
Cool careers without college for people who love to travel / by
Simone Payment.— 1st ed.
    p. cm. — (Cool careers without college)
Summary: Surveys career opportunities for people who are
interested in travel, including adventure travel specialist, cruise
director, flight attendant, deckhand, cruise ship entertainer, tour
guide, and travel agent.
Includes bibliographical references.
ISBN 0-8239-3791-7 (lib. bdg.)
1. Tourism—Vocational guidance—Juvenile literature. [1. Tourism—
Vocational guidance. 2. Vocational guidance.] I. Title. II. Series.
G155.5 .P38 2002
338.4'791023—dc21

                                                            2002006867

Manufactured in the United States of America

CONTENTS

INTRODUCTION

If you're reading this book, you probably already know you like to travel. Maybe you enjoy the excitement of visiting exotic places or meeting new people. Maybe you like to wake up in a different place every day. Or maybe you're drawn to the idea of trying new things: new food, new music, new languages.

Did you ever think that your love of travel could pay the bills? Did you ever consider that you could have a career that would allow you to travel to faraway places—and not just on vacation? There are many careers that allow you to try new things and visit new places. This book will give you some ideas about careers that could help you to lead a life of adventure.

For instance, if you like the water you could become a cruise director on a ship sailing to Hawaii or a deckhand on a fishing boat in Nova Scotia. If you've always wanted to fly, you could take to the skies as a flight attendant. Or you could launch fighter jets from an aircraft carrier stationed off the coast of Saudi Arabia. You could see North America from the cab of a tractor-trailer, or from a speeding passenger train. Are you great behind a camera? Maybe a career as a photojournalist is for you. If you love sports, think about a career as a baseball umpire. As a travel agent you could help other people fulfill their travel dreams—while doing lots of traveling yourself.

These and many other careers described in this book will allow you to see places you might never see otherwise and do things you never thought you'd do. Best of all, they could allow you to do what you love full-time, all year long.

1

ADVENTURE TRAVEL SPECIALIST

Are you ready to lead people on a safari in Africa? Would you like to take a group on a white-water rafting trip in Chile or teach people to hang glide in the Canadian Rockies? If these trips sound good, a job as an adventure travel specialist might be right for you.

Leading adventure travel groups can be a great job for people

A group of adventure tourists enjoys an elephant ride at the Chiang Dao Elephant Camp in Thailand. Camps like this often invite adventure travel specialists on free trips to help them sell the tours.

who like the outdoors and the environment, who enjoy being with groups of people, and who are physically fit. Danielle Wood, who interviewed several adventure travel specialists in her book *The UnCollege Alternative*, says adventure travel offers "constant excitement and a free ticket around the world."

Description

Some adventure travel specialists lead challenging trips to exciting locations. Other adventure travel specialists plan the trips. Some do both the planning and the leading.

Usually, though, even the specialists who only do the planning go on the trips so they can learn about the places that their customers will be visiting and the activities in which they will be participating.

The challenges adventure travel specialists face when on a trip are both physical and mental. They need to have a lot of energy to be able to work hard all day long. They also need to be good, quick thinkers. Adventure travel specialists need to be able to solve many types of problems. They have to stay calm when dealing with emergencies. They need to assess situations to make sure conditions are safe for everyone in the group.

Another important part of the job is working with people. Adventure travel specialists are with their group all day long for several days, or sometimes up to a few weeks, so they need to be comfortable in front of a group. While on the trip they act as a coach and a cheerleader, helping people to face difficult challenges. Adventure travel specialists also need to be good at working on a team and at helping to build teamwork skills in the people they are leading on the trip.

Adventure travel specialists lead people on great adventures, and they just might teach them something along the way. An ocean kayak guide might teach kayaking skills while he or she points out sea life along the way. Adventure travel is sometimes called ecotourism. One of the goals of some adventure travel trips is to teach people

Adventures Aplenty

There are a wide variety of adventure trips that need guides. Here is a small sample of the kinds of trips you could lead:

Land: Backpacking, caving, dogsledding, llama trekking, mountain biking, snowshoeing, wildlife viewing

Water: Fishing, kayaking, scuba diving, snorkeling, surfing, tubing, white-water rafting

Air: Bungee jumping, hang gliding, hot air ballooning, parasailing, skydiving

to appreciate our environment and the plants and animals that live in it.

Education and Training

Most of the time, official training is not needed to become an adventure guide. The best way to prepare for a career as an adventure travel specialist is to gain experience in the type of adventure you'd like to lead. If you'd like to become a white-water rafting guide, go on a rafting trip as a participant and watch carefully what the guide does. Or get a summer job working as an assistant to an experienced guide.

Another way to get experience is by taking a class at a wilderness or adventure school. There are many schools that offer week- or monthlong classes during the summer. Some schools can even train you to become a guide.

Other skills you'll need as a guide are good people skills and good organizational skills. Take public speaking classes so that you become comfortable in front of groups. Join a scouting group or other groups that will help you to build teamwork and outdoor skills. Take first-aid classes so that you'll be prepared for emergencies that can come up, and work on your outdoor cooking skills—most guides have to cook one or more meals a day!

Salary

Salaries can vary for adventure travel specialists. People who work part-time or during only one particular season may make as little as $5,000 per year. But people who work full-time may make more than $65,000. Adventure travel guides often receive tips from satisfied customers. This can add to their income.

Outlook

Adventure travel is one of the fastest growing areas of the travel industry, according to *50 Cutting-Edge Jobs*, edited by Jane Elliot. More people are becoming interested in physical

Adventure tourists share a campfire on a snowmobile safari in Kautokeino Finn, Norway. Leading travel expeditions allows an adventurous person to share his or her love of travel with others.

fitness and in the environment, and they look for trips that combine those two interests. Although jobs in this industry are not always easy to get, people with the right skills should be able to find work.

FOR MORE INFORMATION

ORGANIZATIONS

Adventure Travel Society
332½ W. Sackett Street
Salida, CO 81201
(719) 530-0171
Web site: http://www.adventuretravelbusiness.com
The Adventure Travel Society promotes ecotourism. Their Web site has links to all kinds of information about adventure travel.

America Outdoors®
P.O. Box 10847
Knoxville, TN 37939
(865) 558-3595
e-mail: infoacct@americaoutdoors.org
Web site: http://www.americaoutdoors.org
America Outdoors is an association of companies that provide outdoor recreation services.

The International Ecotourism Society
P.O. Box 668
Burlington, VT 05402
(802) 651-9818
e-mail: ecomail@ecotourism.org
Web site: http://www.ecotourism.org
The International Ecotourism Society is an organization for eco-tourism professionals. Check the Education and Training area of their Web site for information on classes.

Outdoor Industry Association
3775 Iris Avenue, Suite 5
Boulder, CO 80301
(303) 444-3353
e-mail: info@outdoorindustry.org
Web site: http://www.outdoorindustry.org
This association promotes the outdoor recreation industry. Their Web site has plenty of interesting job listings.

SCHOOLS

National Outdoor Leadership School (NOLS)
288 Main Street
Lander, WY 82520-3140
(307) 332-5300
Web site: http://www.nols.edu
NOLS teaches outdoor skills and leadership.

NOLS Professional Training Institute
288 Main Street
Lander, WY 82520-3140
(307) 332-8800
e-mail: pti@nols.edu
Web site: http://pti.nols.edu/

The Professional Training Institute is part of the National Outdoor Leadership School and offers courses to people who want to be instructors and guides.

Outward Bound

(888) 882-6863

Web site: http://www.outwardbound.org/

Outward Bound is a wilderness school with seven locations in the United States. They also offer some classes in other countries. All locations offer courses, and some offer instructor training courses.

Wilderness Medical Associates

189 Dudley Road

Bryant Pond, ME 04219

(888) 945-3633

e-mail: office@wildmed.com

Web site: http://www.wildmed.com

This school offers training for wilderness medical emergencies. They also have a branch in Canada (www.wildmed.ca).

WEB SITES

Adventure Sports Online

http://www.adventuresports.com/

A great, one-stop shop for all types of adventure travel, with information on adventure companies, the gear you'll need, and tips on how to get started in a new sport.

CoolWorks.com

http://www.coolworks.com/

Plenty of links to jobs in travel, resorts, and outdoor adventure travel.

The Outdoor Network

http://outdoornetwork.com/

Information for outdoor industry professionals, including links to jobs, gear, and books.

BOOKS

Doyle, Kevin, Sam Heizmann, and Tanya Stubbs. *The Complete Guide to Environmental Careers in the 21st Century*. Washington, D.C.: Island Press, 1999.
This book has profiles of some people who work as guides. It also has information on other jobs involving the environment.

Eberts, Marjorie, Linda Brothers, and Ann Gisler. *Careers in Travel, Tourism, and Hospitality*. Lincolnwood, IL: VGM Career Horizons, 1997.
An overview of what an adventure travel specialist does is included in this book about travel careers.

Elliot, Jane, ed. *50 Cutting-Edge Jobs*. Chicago, IL: Ferguson Publishing Company, 2000.
This book features a chapter on adventure travel specialists.

Hawks, John K. *Career Opportunities in Travel and Tourism*. New York: Facts On File, Inc., 1995.
Offering a chapter on how to become an adventure tour guide, this book also has general information on travel careers.

Wood, Danielle. *The UnCollege Alternative: Your Guide to Incredible Careers and Amazing Adventures Outside College*. New York: Regan Books, 2000.
This book includes a chapter on getting into adventure travel and covers other alternatives to college.

PERIODICALS

National Geographic Adventure
National Geographic Society
1145 17th Street NW
Washington, D.C. 20036-4688
Web site: http://www.nationalgeographic.com/adventure/
This magazine features stories on outdoor adventure all over the world.

2

AIRCRAFT LAUNCH AND RECOVERY SPECIALIST

"Imagine the rush of a roller-coaster, the heat of a furnace, the blast of 10,000 hair dryers . . . in your face and the sound of every rock and roll band playing right now, all around you, all rolled into one-second-and-a-half action, and that's the launch of one fighter." That's how public relations executive Greg Rubenstein describes his visit to an aircraft carrier to see the launch of F-14 and F-18 fighter jets on the Trans-Am Series Web site (http://www.trans-amseries.com/news/carrier.html). The landing of these jets is just as dramatic. Pilots bring their aircraft in at 120 miles an hour. They have to catch a hook on the tail of the jet onto a cable that brings the plane to a stop in just 200 feet.

Description

An aircraft launch and recovery specialist is in charge of making sure that jets take off and land smoothly and safely. Currently, in the U.S. military this job is open only to men. Working for the U.S. Navy, Coast Guard, or Marine Corps, aircraft launch and recovery specialists are stationed on aircraft carriers all around the world. They operate the catapults that launch the twenty-ton jets into the air at more than 150 miles per hour. They direct the planes on the flight deck with hand or light signals during takeoff and landing. They run the elevators that bring the planes up from the storage deck. They constantly test and check all the equipment involved to make sure it is working well. The safety of the pilots and everyone else on the flight deck is in their hands.

Strict rules are necessary on the flight deck because of the danger involved in takeoffs and landings. Everyone memorizes hand signals so that they can communicate over the roar of the jet engines. Each crewmember has a specific job to do. For a launch, one crewmember hooks the front

An aircraft launch and recovery specialist directs a U.S. marine helicopter as it takes off from the flight deck of the aircraft carrier USS *Juneau*.

wheel of the jet to the catapult. An engineer gives the plane a final check and then gives the pilot the signal to power up the engine. The launch officer gives a signal to the catapult officer. He pushes a button and the jet goes speeding into the air. Everyone is careful to stay out of the way of the jet and the jet's exhaust.

Most aircraft launch and recovery specialists work on aircraft carriers, but some work at landing sites near combat zones. If they are working on land, they install crash barriers and special equipment that helps planes to land and take off on short runways.

Education and Training

A career in the military is one of the best opportunities around. The military can train you for more than 2,000 jobs. You don't have to have any previous experience to join. You can advance within the military, or you can get a job in the civilian work force after you have finished active duty.

To get started in the military, you need a high school diploma and must be seventeen years of age or older. You also must be a U.S. citizen. The first step in joining is to talk to a recruiter. Check your local yellow pages to find a recruiter near you. The recruiter will discuss your options with you. He or she will also talk to you about taking the Armed Services Vocational Aptitude Battery (ASVAB). This test finds your strengths and then gives you a list of areas in which you might do well.

After you have joined the military, you will go to basic training for six to eleven weeks. An aircraft launch and recovery specialist usually trains for nine to thirteen weeks after basic training. That is the time when you will learn about how planes take off and land and how to operate the specialized landing and take-off gear found on an aircraft carrier. You will begin your work as an apprentice, working at all the stations on an aircraft carrier. You will also learn how to repair and maintain equipment. If you are successful in your career, you could move up to crew supervisor or flight deck supervisor.

If you would like to become an aircraft launch and recovery specialist, taking classes in shop mechanics in high

Joining the U.S. military can open the door to careers that you may not have otherwise thought about. Here, landing signal officers monitor the approach of a military jet to the flight deck of an aircraft carrier.

school can help you. Talk to recruiters or other people in the military about what the job is like. They can tell you more about what to expect.

Outlook

The U.S. military hires more than 365,000 people each year, and that number is likely to remain steady. There are about 1,400 aircraft launch and recovery specialists in the military and more than 145,000 people in transportation careers, according to *America's Top Military Careers*.

Salary

A career in the military offers great benefits. The Bureau of Labor Statistics lists $964.80 per month as the current starting salary in the military. You will receive a raise after just four months of service and more raises as you advance. The government pays all food and housing costs. You will also receive full medical and dental benefits, a clothing allowance, and thirty days of vacation per year.

Other Transportation Occupations in the U.S. Military

Here are a few other military careers you might want to consider if you like to travel.

Air crew members operate equipment on board aircraft.

Cargo specialists deliver military supplies, weapons, equipment, and mail all over the world.

Flight engineers monitor aircraft before, during, and after flights.

Seamen operate and maintain military ships and submarines.

Vehicle drivers transport troops, supplies, and fuel.

FOR MORE INFORMATION

ORGANIZATIONS

Canadian Forces Recruiting

(800) 856-8488

Web site: http://www.recruiting.dnd.ca/

Check out their Web site or call for more information on careers in the Canadian army, navy, or air force.

U.S. Coast Guard

(800) GET-USCG (438-8724)

Web site: http://www.uscg.mil

Full information about careers in the Coast Guard can be found on their Web site or at their toll-free number.

U.S. Marine Corps

(800) MARINES (627-4637)

Web site: http://www.marines.com

Information about the Marines can be found on their Web site, or by calling their toll-free number.

U.S. Navy

(800) USA-NAVY (872-6289)

Web site: http://www.navy.mil

Call or check out their Web site for information on careers and getting started in the navy.

WEB SITES

Armed Forces Careers.com
http://www.armedforcescareers.com/
Information on enlisting, choosing a branch of the military, and taking the ASVAB can be found here.

Canadian National Defence
http://www.recruiting.dnd.ca/html/index.html
This Canadian military site can help you find jobs that match your interests.

F-16.net
http://www.f-16.net/ground.html
This Web site, focused on the F-16 fighter jet, has a "day in the life" description of how an F-16 is prepared, launched, and refueled.

Military Career Guide Online
http://www.militarycareers.com/index.html
This official U.S. government Web site is a full guide to all careers in the military. Check the URL below for more information on careers in transportation.
http://64.124.146.114/occ/meotrans.htm

NOVA: Aircraft Carrier
http://www.pbs.org/wgbh/nova/transcripts/2110gairc.html
The transcript of the *NOVA* television program "Aircraft Carrier" is available here. The program tours the USS *Independence* to show what life is like on an aircraft carrier at sea.

NTB Trans-Am Series
http://www.trans-amseries.com/news/carrier.html
This diary of a visit to an aircraft carrier provides details about what life is like on an aircraft carrier.

BOOKS

Hutton, Donald B. *Guide to Military Careers*. Hauppauge, NY: Barron's Educational Series, Inc., 1998.
This book provides a general guide to careers in the military.

Ostrow, Scott. *Everything You Need to Score High on the ASVAB.* Seventeenth ed. Denver, CO: Arco Publishers, Inc., 2001.
This guide contains tips on taking the ASVAB exam and includes practice tests.

Ostrow, Scott. *A Guide to Joining the Military.* Lawrenceville, NJ: Thomson Learning, 2000.
This book provides information that will help you to decide if a career in the military is right for you.

Roza, Greg. *Choosing a Career in the Military.* New York: The Rosen Publishing Group, Inc., 2001.
Learn whether a career in the military is right for you in this overview.

United States Department of Defense, compiler. *America's Top Military Careers.* Indianapolis, IN: JIST Works, Inc., 2000.
Detailed information about most of the careers offered in the military can be found in this book.

Wood, Danielle. *The UnCollege Alternative: Your Guide to Incredible Careers and Amazing Adventures Outside College.* New York: Regan Books, 2000.
This book includes a chapter on careers in the military and covers other alternatives to college.

VIDEOS
"Aircraft Carrier"
A *NOVA* television program from PBS that shows what life is like on the aircraft carrier USS *Independence*. To order call 1-800-949-8670, ext. 498.

3

BASEBALL UMPIRE

The bases are loaded and there are two outs. The home team is down by one run and there's a full count on the batter at the plate. You're behind the plate ready to call the next pitch. You call it a strike—the batter is out and the game is finished. The crowd boos, the players yell, and the manager storms out of the dugout. You're the umpire, and you stay calm. You know you have made the right call.

A baseball umpire motions the safe call as a baserunner slides into home plate. Umpires not only get to be eyewitnesses to great plays, they also get to travel to the major league cities of the United States and Canada.

Being an umpire is not an easy job. Barry Mano, the president of the National Association of Sports Officials says, "[I]t takes a special person—a person with integrity, courage, and good judgment." For information on jobs officiating other sports, check out the association's Web site (http://www.naso.org).

Description

An umpire's main duty is to make sure that players follow the rules of the game. Umpires also keep official records and resolve any arguments that come up during the game.

Umpires must be able to concentrate. There is "no time for daydreaming in this position—looking away for even one second can mean missing important action" writes Shelly Field in *Career Opportunities in the Sports Industry*. An umpire also needs to remain calm and professional at all times.

During the season, umpires travel a great deal. Professional umpires in the major and minor leagues have all their travel expenses and meals paid for. Major league umpires get to fly first class.

Umpires have to deal with many of the same things as players do. Games are often scheduled on weekends and evenings and sometimes holidays. Many games are held outside—even if it is very hot, very cold, or very rainy. Umpires are on their feet for the whole game, which usually lasts around three hours. But, like players, umpires have many months off during the winter.

Education and Training

Most umpires get their start by working at local recreation program games, middle school games, or high school games. To get started at this level, talk to local officials and contact associations such as the National Association of Sports Officials. With some experience, an umpire can move up to working at college games.

Umpire trainees practice the "out" signal at the Joe Brinkman umpire school in St. Petersburg, Florida.

Once you have had some experience and have learned the rules of the game, there are two schools you can attend (see For More Information). Both schools offer courses during the winter. Classes last about five weeks. The best students at these schools are invited to stay for an extra week to be evaluated. The very best students in that group are then hired by the minor leagues.

Professional umpires work their way up through the leagues much as players usually do. According to Tom Leppard, the Major League Baseball director of umpire administration, it usually takes from seven to ten years in the minor leagues for an umpire to reach the major leagues.

In addition to attending one of the two umpire schools, a potential umpire needs a high school degree or GED, good eyesight, quick reflexes, and good coordination. An umpire must be able to remain calm in stressful situations, and, of course, he or she always has to be fair.

Salary

Salaries for umpires depend on the level of baseball for which they are working. Class A minor league umpires make $1,900–$2,200 per month. Umpires in Class AAA minor leagues make $2,500–$3,400 per month. Major league umpires make up to $280,000 per year. In addition, major league umpires who work in play-off games get $17,500, and those who work the World Series earn $20,000, according to the Wendelstedt Umpire School Web site.

Outlook

The National Association of Sports Officials says that there is a need for officials at every level of competition. There are plenty of opportunities for part-time umpires at the high school level. There are also jobs at the college and

Baseball Umpire Famous Firsts

Here are some famous firsts in umpiring. You can find more on the Major League Baseball Web site (http://www.mlb.com).

1876 - William McLean became the first professional umpire when he umpired the first game in National League history between Boston and Philadelphia on April 22.

1903 - Hank O'Day and Thomas Connolly worked the first modern World Series, which pitted the Boston Pilgrims against the Pittsburgh Pirates.

1951 - Emmett Ashford became the first African American professional umpire when he began working in the Southwestern International League.

1972 - Bernice Gera became the first woman to umpire a professional baseball game when she worked a Class A New York–Penn League game.

semiprofessional level. Just as it is difficult for a baseball player to get all the way to the major leagues, it is difficult for umpires to get a job in the major leagues. However, with talent and hard work it is possible.

FOR MORE INFORMATION

ORGANIZATIONS

National Association of Sports Officials (NASO)
2017 Lathrop Avenue
Racine, WI 53405
(262) 632-5448
e-mail: cservice@naso.org
Web site: http://www.naso.org/
NASO is a national organization for sports officials from all levels and all sports. Their Web site offers all kinds of information on getting started in sports officiating and has links to local and national associations.

National Federation of State High School Associations (NFSHA)
690 Washington Street
Indianapolis, IN 46204
(317) 972-6900
Web site: http://www.nfhs.org
Contact the NFSHA for information on officiating high school baseball games.

The Professional Baseball Umpire Corporation (PBUC)
P.O. Box A
St. Petersburg, FL 33731
(727) 822-6937
Web site: http://www.minorleaguebaseball.com/
The PBUC trains and evaluates all umpires in the Minor League Baseball system in the United States and Canada. They decide who will advance within the minor league and who will move up to the major leagues.

SCHOOLS

Jim Evans Academy of Professional Umpiring
12741 Research Boulevard, Suite 401
Austin, TX 78759
(512) 335-5959
e-mail: jimsacademy@earthlink.net
Web site: http://www.umpireacademy.com
This is one of two professional umpire schools.

Wendelstedt Umpire School
88 South St. Andrews Drive
Ormond Beach, FL 32174
(386) 672-4879
e-mail: umpsch@aol.com
Web site: http://www.umpireschool.com
This is one of two professional umpire schools.

WEB SITES

Baseball Umpires
http://www.baseballumpires.com
This is a Web site for professional umpires with links to official rules of the game, FAQs, a newsletter, and links to other sites.

Major League Baseball.com
http://www2.mlb.com/NASApp/mlb/mlb/official_info/mlb_umpires.jsp
The umpire section of the Major League Baseball site has information on rules of the game, biographies of current major league umpires, and interesting articles. Be sure to check out the overview of how to become an umpire.

National Association of Sports Officials (NASO): Becoming a Sports Official
http://www.naso.org/BeOfficial/bofficial.htm
This branch of the NASO site gives you information about what being a sports official is like and tells you how to get started in your career.

Referee
http://www.referee.com/
The online version of *Referee* magazine offers some articles and tips from recent issues. Also look for the link to the Sports Officiating Resource Center for Education (SORCE) that offers a catalog of books and videos on officiating.

BOOKS

Field, Shelly. *Career Opportunities in the Sports Industry.* 2nd ed. New York: Checkmark Books, 1999.
This book provides advice for becoming an umpire as well as information on other careers in sports.

Savage, Jim. *A Career in Professional Sports.* Minneapolis, MN: Capstone Press, 1996.
Includes descriptions of careers relating to sports, including athlete, coach, official, marketing, and team management.

PERIODICALS

Referee
P.O. Box 161
Franksville, WI 53126
(262) 632-8855
e-mail: questions@referee.com
Web site: http://www.referee.com/
Referee magazine is written by and for sports officials and offers articles, tips, and information on training. Check out their Web site for subscription information and some articles from recent issues.

VIDEOS

You Have to Love It When They Boo!
This twelve-minute video shows you what the life of an official is like. It is available from the National Association of Sports Officials (NASO) Web site (www.naso.org), by phone (800-733-6100), fax (262-632-5460) or e-mail (naso@naso.org).

4

CRUISE DIRECTOR

It's 6:30 AM and you're in a meeting with the ship's captain. At 7:30 you're greeting guests at breakfast. It's 8:15 and you're in your office meeting with your staff. By 9:30 you're checking to make sure guests have gotten safely to shore. At 9:45 you're answering a question from a passenger. Next comes a question from one of your staff. And then you're off to a bingo game. Your busy morning continues, and then it's time for lunch. The afternoon passes in a blur, and the evening is no different. Soon it is 11:30 PM and you collapse into your bed. Your busy day is finally finished.

This sounds like a long day and it is. But did we mention that this long day took place on a cruise ship sailing off the coast of Mexico? A cruise director's job can be tiring, but there are many advantages. Your room on the ship is free and you eat great meals at any time of day—also for free. Maybe best of all, you are seeing the world from the deck of a beautiful ship.

Description

Mary Fallon Miller, a cruise line travel agent, calls a cruise director a "combination of manager, entertainer, cheerleader, and friend." He or she plans all the activities and entertainment on the ship. There are all kinds of activities to plan: sports, movies, trips to shore, special dinners, and evening entertainment. The cruise director often hosts or introduces the shows each night. Maybe the most important job a cruise director has is making sure the passengers are happy.

A cruise director fields a question from a passenger during the welcoming session at the beginning of a cruise.

Being a cruise director is a very demanding job. You often work from ten to fifteen hours per day for many days in a row. You need to get along well with all kinds of people and be polite even if a passenger is complaining. Even when you are not on duty, you have to be friendly to passengers.

Most people do not begin their cruise ship careers as a cruise director. It is a job that requires a lot of experience. Many people start as an assistant cruise director or have another job on the cruise director's staff. See the sidebar below for other jobs that are good places to get started on your cruise director career.

You're Not Alone

There are many people on the cruise director's staff. Working for a cruise director as a staff member is a great way to learn. Here are some jobs you could do to gain experience:

Assistant cruise director: helps the cruise director plan activities, makes up the daily schedule

Cruise staff: does a wide variety of jobs, helps out with activities and games

DJ: works with the cruise director to plan theme nights

Shore excursion manager: organizes trips off the ship

Social host/hostess: greets and socializes with guests

Education and Training

Cruise directors have to be focused on customer service. They need to be creative, organized, energetic, flexible, and, most of all, friendly. You can't take a class to become any of those things. There are things you can do to prepare for a career as a cruise director, though. Take public speaking classes so that you become comfortable talking in front of groups. Help plan a school trip so that you can find out what scheduling and leading groups of people involves. Learning a foreign language can also be helpful.

Do research on what cruise ships are like and what kinds of jobs are available. Try talking to travel agents or people who have worked on ships. Read travel magazines or the travel section of the newspaper. That way you can find out if a cruise line is adding a new ship and will need to hire new people.

You can also consider going to a travel school. The American Society of Travel Agents lists travel schools on their Web site (http://www.astanet.com). There are many travel programs around the country. Some of them specialize in training people for cruise ship jobs.

Salary

JobMonkey.com lists salaries for cruise directors at more than $80,000 per year. An assistant cruise director earns

As host, the cruise director often checks on passengers to see if they are having a good time.

about $48,000 per year. While you are on the ship all your expenses are paid. You also have free medical care and a clothing allowance.

Outlook

In 2000, 6.9 million passengers sailed on cruise ships, according to the International Council of Cruise Lines, and even more are expected in the coming years. On many cruise ships, there is one crewmember for every two or three passengers, so you can see that many crewmembers are needed. The Bureau of Labor Statistics expects the cruise industry to keep growing. New cruise ships are being built over the next three or four years. This will create many new jobs.

Although a job as a cruise director is not easy to get, you can work your way up to that position. Many people leave the cruise industry after a few years, or take a break from it, so there are often job openings.

FOR MORE INFORMATION

ORGANIZATIONS

American Society of Travel Agents (ASTA)
1101 King Street, Suite 200
Alexandria, VA 22314
(703) 739-2782
Web site: http://www.astanet.com
ASTA is the leading organization for travel professionals. Check the Education/Careers section of the Web site to get information on travel schools. You can search for schools that specialize in cruises.

Cruise Lines International Association (CLIA)
500 Fifth Avenue, Suite 1407
New York, NY 10110
(212) 921-0066
e-mail: info@cruising.org
Web site: http://www.cruising.org
CLIA is the official organization of the cruise industry. They work with cruise lines and travel agents.

Institute of Certified Travel Agents (ICTA)
148 Linden Street
Wellesley, MA 02482
(800) 542-4282
Web site: http://www.icta.com
ICTA trains and certifies travel professionals. Their Web site can help you find schools near you and can help you plan your travel career.

International Council of Cruise Lines (ICCL)
2111 Wilson Boulevard, 8th Floor
Arlington, VA 22201
(800) 595-9338
e-mail: info@iccl.org
Web site: http://www.iccl.org
The ICCL provides information on its members, which include many of the major cruise lines. They also do research on the cruise industry.

WEB SITES

CoolWorks.com
http://www.coolworks.com
Check the Jobs on Water section for links to cruise ship jobs.

Cruise Ship Database
http://www.jcoston.bizland.com/cruisedbfr.html
This database provides complete address information for cruise ship companies based in the United States and abroad.

Hcareers.com
http://www.hcareers.com
Hcareers.com lists hotel, restaurant, and cruise ship jobs. Jobs in Canada can be found here: http://www.hcareers.ca

JobMonkey.com
http://www.jobmonkey.com/cruise
This site has excellent information about getting into the cruise industry and has job postings.

Resort Jobs.com
http://www.resortjobs.com/do/where
This site features links to cruise and resort jobs worldwide. Check the Resources section for links to internship and summer job opportunities.

BOOKS

Eberts, Marjorie, Linda Brothers, and Ann Gisler. *Careers in Travel, Tourism, and Hospitality*. Lincolnwood, IL: VGM Career Horizons, 1997. An overview of careers in the cruise industry is included in this book about travel careers.

Marin, Richard B. *Cruise Ship Jobs: The Insiders Guide to Finding and Getting Jobs on Cruise Ships Around the World*. Coconut Creek, FL: Portofino Publications, 1998.
You can find detailed information on being a cruise director in this book. It also contains answers to many common questions about life on cruise ships.

Miller, Mary Fallon. *How to Get a Job with a Cruise Line*. Fourth ed. St. Petersburg, FL: Ticket to Adventure, Inc., 1997.
This book contains practical information on how to get a job on a cruise ship. It also features profiles of people who have held cruise ship jobs.

PERIODICALS

Travel Weekly
(800) 360-0015
e-mail: twcrossroads@cahners.com
Web site: http://www.twcrossroads.com
Travel Weekly is a good magazine to read to learn about the travel industry.

Cruise Travel
990 Grove Street
Evanston, IL 60201-4370
Web site: http://cruisetravelmag.com/
Read this magazine to get general information on cruises.

5

DECKHAND

Do you love being on the water? Would you like to spend your days fishing on the open sea, drifting down the Mississippi on a riverboat, or crossing the Pacific Ocean on a cruise ship? Deckhands work on many types of boats, including cruise ships, cargo ships, fishing boats, barges, riverboats, and ferries. Some deckhands even work on luxury yachts on round-the-world trips.

Description

Most deckhand positions involve helping out on a boat. Deckhands can get jobs on many different types of boats, so specific duties can vary. On commercial fishing boats, deckhands operate the fishing gear (such as nets and fishing line) and help to haul the fish into the boat. Once the fish are on the boat, deckhands clean and salt the fish and put the catch on ice for the long trip back to land.

Deckhand jobs on cruise ships are not easy to get because most cruise ships hire crewmembers who are not American. However, small cruise ships and riverboats do hire American deckhands. On a riverboat or cruise ship, a deckhand does everything from painting and cleaning to helping dock the boat.

On cargo ships, deckhands (sometimes also called seamen) perform many jobs. They sometimes steer the ship or stand watch—looking out for other ships and making sure the ship is on course. They help dock the ship when it lands. They may help load or unload cargo and may keep track of cargo during the ship's journey. Deckhands also make sure the ship is clean and in good working order.

Deckhands who work on private boats or yachts help to sail the boat and make sure it is clean and running well. On boats with a small crew, deckhands sometimes also have other duties, such as cooking. Passenger ferries hire

Deckhands perform various odd jobs on a boat or ship. Here a deck-hand unspools a roll of cable on a pipe-laying barge.

deckhands to help dock the boat, load cars and passengers, and collect money from passengers.

Being a deckhand can be dangerous. Weather conditions can sometimes be harsh. If the boat has a problem and is far from land, the crew needs to solve the problem on their own because there is no one else to help them. There is also the risk of falling overboard, particularly on a fishing boat or large cargo ship.

Some types of boats may be at sea—and away from land—for weeks or months at a time. Deckhands who work on cargo ships, fishing boats, or cruise ships usually work for several months at a time, and then have a month or two off. While they are at sea they might be on duty for four hours, then off duty for eight hours, seven days a week. Deckhands on passenger ferries or boats in rivers and harbors usually have a much more regular work schedule. They might work eight- or twelve-hour shifts, five days a week. Or they may work steadily for a week and then have a week off.

Education and Training

Most deckhands receive on-the-job training. Experience on boats is the most important requirement for getting hired for many deckhand jobs. Some jobs on cargo ships or cruise ships require the deckhand to be licensed by the U.S. Coast Guard.

There are schools that can train you for a career as a deckhand. You can also take courses sponsored by the U.S. Coast Guard or Canadian Coast Guard. Some companies have their own school and will train you when you are hired.

Another great way to get experience is in the U.S. military. The U.S. Army, Navy, Marine Corps, and Coast Guard have many careers that will prepare you for deckhand jobs. Check the Military Career Guide online for more information (http://www.militarycareers.com/index.html).

To obtain most deckhand jobs, you will need to be healthy and strong for the physically demanding duties.

Patience is helpful because days at sea can be long, and there are times when you are not on duty and there is little to do. A deckhand must be flexible enough to step in and do another crew member's job if someone is sick or injured. Being able to work on a team is a very important quality for any deckhand. Crews must work together well so that everyone on board remains safe.

Salary

Salaries for deckhands also vary. Workers on fishing boats make between $300 and $750 per week, according to the Bureau of Labor Statistics. Salaries for workers on fishing boats vary according to the season, and depend on how many fish are caught on a trip. Water transportation workers earn about $11.70 per hour. Pay varies for deckhands who work on small cruise ships and yachts.

Outlook

The outlook for deckhand jobs varies. Jobs on cruise ships will probably increase over the next few years. Deckhand jobs on fishing boats and cargo ships may decline slightly.

Two deckhands assist a captain as he works on a tugboat. There is really no specific job description for deckhand beyond lending a hand where needed, but the job often involves hard work.

FOR MORE INFORMATION

ORGANIZATIONS

Canadian Coast Guard

Fisheries & Oceans Canada Communications Branch
200 Kent Street
13th Floor, Station 13228
Ottawa, Ontario, Canada K1A 0E6
(613) 993-0999
Web site: http://www.ccg-gcc.gc.ca/main_e.htm
The Canadian Coast Guard has fishery information and has a college that can train you for a shipboard career.

Maritime Administration

U.S. Department of Transportation
400 7th Street SW, Room 7302
Washington, DC 20590
(800) 996-2723
Web site: http://www.marad.dot.gov
Information on merchant marine careers, training, and licensing requirements is available from this branch of the U.S. Department of Transportation.

Seafarers' International Union

5201 Auth Way
Camp Springs, MD 20746
(301) 899-0675
Web site: http://www.seafarers.org/index.html
This union represents engineers, stewards, and deckhands on ships. They have job listings on their Web site.

U.S. Coast Guard
(800) GET-USCG (438-8724)
Web site: http://www.uscg.mil
Joining the Coast Guard can train you for a career aboard a ship.

SCHOOLS

Paul Hall Center for Maritime Training and Education
P.O. Box 75
Piney Point, MD 20674-0075
(877) 235-3275
Web site: http://www.seafarers.org/phc
This school prepares students for many shipboard careers. The school guarantees a job to students who complete their entry-level training program.

Sea Education Association (SEA)
P.O. Box 6
Woods Hole, MA 02543
(800) 552-3633
Web site: http://www.sea.edu/default.htm
SEA has classes for high school and college students to learn about life at sea. They also have job opportunities listed on their Web site.

WEB SITES

BoatCrewsUSA.com
http://www.boatcrewsusa.com/contents.htm
This site has listings for many jobs in the marine industry. Fill out an online application and learn about opportunities around the world.

CoolWorks.com
http://www.coolworks.com/jobs-on-water.htm
Find jobs on cruise ships, fishing boats, yachts, and riverboats on this site.

International Seafarers Exchange
http://www.jobxchange.com
In addition to job listings, this site has good descriptions of ship jobs. Be sure to check the Work Aboard section for tips on preparing for a maritime career.

JobMonkey.com
http://www.jobmonkey.com/alaska
JobMonkey gives you a good overview of opportunities in the Alaska fishing industry. They also have job listings.

BOOKS

Farr, J. Michael. *America's Top Jobs for People Without a Four-Year Degree.* Fifth ed. Indianapolis, IN: JIST Works, Inc., 2001.
You can get a good overview of fishing jobs and other water transportation jobs in this career guide.

Junger, Sebastian. *The Perfect Storm: A True Story of Men Against the Sea*. New York: Harper Mass Market Paperbacks, 1998.
This book, which was made into a movie, describes the danger and excitement of life on a fishing boat.

Winters, Adam. *Choosing a Career in the Fishing Industry*. New York: The Rosen Publishing Group, Inc., 2000.
Find out if life in the fishing industry is for you in this overview of fishing careers.

PERIODICALS

Professional Mariner
Web site: http://www.professionalmariner.com
This magazine and its online version have information on commercial and military ships and career information.

6

FLIGHT ATTENDANT

Would you like to wake up in New York City and go to sleep in Paris, France? As a flight attendant, you could do that on a regular basis. Having a job as a flight attendant is nothing like having a 9-to-5 job in an office. It can be glamorous, with layovers in exotic locations and many days off. It's also a lot of hard work with long hours. If you are flexible, love to meet people from all over the

A flight attendant demonstrates the use of passenger emergency gear during takeoff. Flight attendants are concerned with the comfort and safety of passengers during flight.

world, and enjoy taking off at a moment's notice, a job as a flight attendant might be for you.

Description

If you've flown on an airplane, you've seen flight attendants greeting passengers at the door and getting bags safely packed into the storage bins. A flight attendant instructed you on safety procedures and probably served you drinks and a meal.

The duties you see a flight attendant performing on a routine flight are a big part of the job, but flight attendants do much more. Before a flight they make sure the plane is ready for passengers. Flight attendants help people in emergency situations and answer questions during flights. Flight attendants often work long days, and those days can become much longer if there is bad weather or a problem with the plane. They usually are on duty for more than one flight per day, and often work nights, weekends, or holidays. Most flight attendants fly from seventy-five to eighty-five hours per month and spend another seventy-five to eighty-five hours working on the ground preparing planes or doing paperwork after a flight. Airlines usually have a maximum number of hours a flight attendant can fly in a month. Once the maximum number of hours is reached, a flight attendant will have the rest of the month off. Sometimes a flight attendant can have as many as ten days off in a row.

Usually flight attendants start their careers on reserve. This means that they have scheduled days off, and scheduled days on. They can get called at any time on their days on. They need to be able to get to the airport—ready to fly—within an hour or two. Most flight attendants live near the airport where they are based so that they'll be able to get there quickly.

Education and Training

Airlines usually look for men and women who are healthy, clean-cut, mature, dependable, and friendly. Flight attendants

A flight crew practices emergency evacuation on a United Boeing 767 flight simulator. Flight attendants are responsible for guiding passengers during emergencies such as a crash landing.

need to be flexible, have a positive attitude, and be ready to deal with any kind of situation. One of their most important jobs is dealing with passengers, so experience dealing with all kinds of people is very important.

A high school diploma or GED is required to get a job as a flight attendant. Most airlines like to hire people who are at least from eighteen to twenty-one years of age. Some college education is preferred, but not necessary. It's a good idea to have first-aid training and experience with public speaking. Any customer experience is good, such as waitressing or working in a hotel. Volunteer work as a tour guide

Corporate Travel: An Alternative to Airlines

Flying for the airlines is not your only option as a flight attendant. Large corporations that have their own airplanes often hire flight attendants. Michelle Graziano was a corporatc flight attcndant for three years. She says it's a great way to see the world. She was able to fly on a round-the-world trip once a year and had time off to explore places like China and South America. Corporate flight attendants wear beepers when on call and need to be able to get the plane ready to go on a moment's notice.

or in a hospital can help to show an airline that you are skilled at working with people.

Michelle Graziano, who worked for a major airline and in corporate travel, recommends learning a second language or studying abroad. She also suggests working for an airline's frequent traveler lounge. That will give you a chance to see how the airlines work and will give you good customer service experience.

When you are ready to apply for a job at an airline, be aggressive and persistent. Michelle Graziano recommends talking to someone who already works for an airline to find out what the airline looks for when it is hiring. She may also be able to tell you what kinds of questions to expect in an interview. She also recommends going to open houses that airlines host in various cities. If the airline thinks you are a good candidate, they will fly you to their base city for an interview.

If you are hired by an airline, they will train you for four to six weeks. They teach you first aid and emergency procedures, how to deal with difficult passengers, and how to serve food and drinks. Near the end of your training you go on several practice flights.

Salary

Many flight attendants belong to unions so they have good benefits and salary. Most earn between $28,000 and $56,000 per year, according to the Bureau of Labor Statistics. One of the benefits of being a flight attendant is free or discounted travel. Flight attendants usually get free flights on the airline that they work for, and sometimes on other airlines. They often get discounts on hotels, cruises, and rental cars as well. Often the family members of flight attendants also get discounts on travel.

Outlook

There should be good opportunities for flight attendants over the next ten years. The number of jobs changes depending on the U.S. economy, but overall there are expected to be more flight jobs in the coming years, according to the Bureau of Labor Statistics.

FOR MORE INFORMATION

ORGANIZATIONS
Air Transport Association (ATA)
1301 Pennsylvania Avenue NW, Suite 1100
Washington, DC 20004-1707
(202) 626-4000
Web site: http://www.airlines.org/public/home/default1.asp
Most major airlines belong to the ATA. The ATA has a brochure called "People of the Airlines" that lists the names, addresses, and phone numbers of its member airlines. You can get a free copy of this brochure by writing to the Public Information Department at the address above.

Association of Flight Attendants (AFA)
1275 K Street NW, Suite 500
Washington, DC 20005
(202) 712-9799
e-mail: afatalk@afanet.org
Web site: http://www.flightattendant-afa.org
The AFA is a union that helps organize flight attendants from many airlines. They help flight attendants get better pay and benefits.

FlightSafety International
Cabin Attendant Training
301 Robert B. Miller Road
Savannah, GA 31408
(800) 625-9369
Web site: http://www.flightsafety.com
FlightSafety International trains flight attendants for corporate or commercial travel.

Jet Professionals, Inc.
114 Charles Lindbergh Drive
Teterboro, NJ 07608
(800) 441-6016
Web site: http://www.jet-professionals.com/index.htm
Jet Professionals is a placement agency that deals mostly with corporate travel.

WEB SITES

AirlineCareer.com
http://www.airlinecareer.com
This Web site has articles written by flight attendants that give you an idea of what it is like to fly.

Avjobs.com
http://www.avjobs.com/careers/flightattendant
Avjobs helps people find jobs in the airline industry. Their Web site has a career guide that describes requirements for flight attendants and has information on corporate flight attendants.

Beyond and Above
http://www.beyondandabove.net/index.html
This Web site gives information and opportunities regarding corporate flight attendant training. Courses are also offered.

FlightAttendants.org
http://www.flightattendants.org
This Web site features information for getting started on your flight attendant career.

BOOKS

Bock, Becky. *Welcome Aboard! Your Career as a Flight Attendant.* Aurora, CO: Cage Consulting, Inc., 1998.
This book has a good description of what a flight attendant does and provides practical advice on preparing for a career as a flight attendant.

Kirkwood, Tim. *Flight Attendant Job Finder and Career Guide.* River Forest, IL: Planning/Communications, 1999.
You'll find advice on how to get a job as a flight attendant and specific information on U.S. and Canadian airlines in this guide.

Krannich, Ronald, and Caryl Rae Krannich. *The Best Jobs for the 21st Century.* Third ed. Manassas Park, VA: Impact Publications, 1998.
This book includes an overview of a career as a flight attendant.

Rule, Luauna. *An Insider's Secrets to Becoming a Flight Attendant.* Littleton, CO: Flight Attendant Corporation of America, 1997.
You can find information that will help you decide if a career as a flight attendant is right for you. This book also includes advice on applying, interviewing, and training for flight attendant jobs.

7

LONG-HAUL TRUCK DRIVER

The motto of the Professional Truck Driver Institute is "If someone has it, a truck brought it," and, as a long-haul trucker, you could bring it to them. While you're bringing it to them you'll get a chance to see parts of the country you might never see otherwise. Although you have a schedule you need to keep, you get to be your own boss and are certainly never stuck in an office.

Description

Truck drivers are responsible for getting their cargo to its destination safely and on time. Before a trip, the driver checks the truck and cargo to make sure that everything is in good shape. When the trucker reaches the delivery location he or she sometimes helps to unload the cargo and then fills out paperwork about his or her trip.

Some truck drivers work for a trucking company and have regular routes. Tim James, who works for a trucking company, has a regular route and gets to be home two times a week. Other drivers may be sent on different routes every time they make a trip. Sometimes truckers drive in teams, with one sleeping while the other is driving.

Some drivers work in trucks that they own. Owners are responsible for making all payments related to the truck, which can be expensive. They must keep their truck in good condition and take as many jobs as possible in order to turn a profit. When Tim James drove his own truck, he was away from home for four to six weeks at a time.

Trucks today are much safer—and more comfortable—than they were twenty years ago. Most trucks have cabins with TVs, computers, DVD players, microwaves, ovens, refrigerators, and two beds. Most of the time truckers sleep in their own trucks, unless the weather is bad. Some trucks have global positioning systems (GPS) that tell them exactly where they are at all times and help them to communicate with their dispatcher.

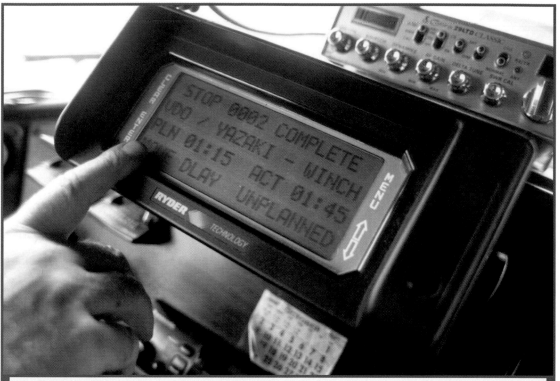

A truck driver checks for travel information on an on-board computer. Today's trucks are fitted with computer and personal electronics devices to make them safer and more comfortable than they used to be.

Education and Training

One of the main requirements for a truck driver is being a better-than-average driver. You'll be responsible for delivering your cargo safely. And of course you must love to drive because that's what you'll be doing all day long.

If you're thinking about a career in long-haul trucking, you might want to take driver training and auto mechanic classes in high school. Some technical and vocational schools offer training courses for truck drivers. Usually when you are hired by a trucking company they will send you to school, so taking classes on your own is not always necessary.

Before you can drive for a long-haul trucking company, you will need to get a commercial driver's license (CDL). To get a license you need to pass the CDL exam, which has a written test and a driving test. Trucking schools will help you to prepare for the exam. There are also books that can help you study (see the For More Information section).

Most trucking companies require drivers to be at least twenty-three years old to drive tractor-trailers. A good way to get experience before you are twenty-three is with companies that make local deliveries within a city or state. Sometimes younger drivers can work as a truck driver's helper. Helpers drive part of the time and may help load and unload the truck.

Another good way to get experience is by joining the military. Almost all branches of the military need drivers. See the Military Career Guide online for more information (http://www.militarycareers.com/index.html).

Salary

Truck drivers who drive tractor-trailers usually earn between $12 and $19 an hour. These drivers are usually paid by the mile. If drivers own their own trucks, they usually make between $20,000 and $50,000 per year, after they pay their expenses, according to the Bureau of Labor Statistics.

Drivers who work for local delivery companies usually earn between $8 and $15 per hour. These drivers are usually

A female gas truck driver delivers gasoline to a gas station in Honolulu, Hawaii, using a flexible pipe to connect her truck to a station's tank. In recent years, more and more women have become truckers.

paid by the hour and get overtime if they work more than forty hours per week.

Outlook

There will be many opportunities for truck drivers to get jobs in the coming years. Trucks can often deliver cargo faster than railroads and other types of transportation, so the industry is expected to grow.

Profile

INTERVIEW WITH TIM JAMES

Tim James has driven trucks all across the United States.

WHAT DO YOU LIKE BEST ABOUT YOUR JOB?

The best thing is seeing different cultures, scenery, and landmarks. I've seen things I probably never would have seen otherwise. I always say that I am not a professional driver, I'm a professional tourist.

ARE THERE THINGS YOU DON'T LIKE ABOUT LONG-HAUL TRUCKING?

The loneliness is difficult. Also, it's not an easy life if you're married and have children. You are away from home a lot and sometimes you miss Christmas, or your children's birthdays, or your wedding anniversary.

WHAT ADVICE DO YOU HAVE FOR PEOPLE WHO WOULD LIKE TO GET INTO TRUCKING?

You can get your start working for local trucking companies, making deliveries. This gives you good experience with traffic, and you learn how to maneuver your truck in traffic. When you are twenty-three you can get a job with a long-haul company. They will send you to a school to learn how to operate a truck and prepare for the CDL exam.

FOR MORE INFORMATION

ORGANIZATIONS

Ontario Trucking Association

555 Dixon Road
Toronto, Ontario, Canada M9W 1H8
(416) 249-7401
e-mail: info@ontruck.org
Web site: http://www.ontruck.org
The Ontario Trucking Association provides information to truckers working in North America.

Professional Truck Driver Institute, Inc. (PTDI)

2200 Mill Road
Alexandria, VA 22314
(703) 838-8842
e-mail: ptdi@truckload.org
Web site: http://www.ptdi.org
PTDI was organized to make sure that new truck drivers learn the rules and regulations of trucking.

Trucker Buddy International

P.O. Box 527
Waupaca, WI 54981
(800) MY-BUDDY (692-8339)
e-mail: info@truckerbuddy.org
Web site: http://www.truckerbuddy.org/tbihomepage.asp
Trucker Buddy matches professional truck drivers with schoolchildren to teach them about life on the road. Check their Web site to see how

you can get your school matched with a truck driver. Be sure to follow the links to Trucker Buddy Web sites for diaries and other information from truckers.

WEB SITES

BestDriverJobs.com
http://www.bestdriverjobs.com
This site features many jobs in the trucking industry.

eTrucker.com
http://www.etrucker.com
This is the online version of *Truckers News* magazine. It has news, articles, online bulletin boards to communicate with other truckers, and links to information on schools and jobs.

Professional Truck Driver Institute, Inc. (PTDI)
http://www.ptdi.org/
In addition to general information about trucking, this site provides a full list of schools with certified courses and links to job postings.

Truckinginfo.com
http://www.truckinginfo.com
Trucking information and news can be found here, along with job postings.

WhoHasJobs.com
http://www.whohasjobs.com/field/019/index.htm
This site has many listings for trucking jobs, as well as other jobs in transportation.

BOOKS

Farr, J. Michael. *America's Top Jobs for People without a Four-Year Degree.* Fifth ed. Indianapolis, IN: JIST Works, Inc., 2001.
This book provides a general overview of trucking and has information on other careers that do not require a college degree.

Professional Truck Driver Institute of America. *Trucking: Tractor-Trailer Driver Handbook/Workbook*. Orange, CA: Career Publishing Incorporated, 1997.
You'll find everything you need to know about becoming a truck driver and about the trucking industry in this book.

Research and Education Association. *The Best Home Study Guide for the Commercial Driver License Exam*. Piscataway, NJ: Research and Education Association, 2001.
This guide helps you to prepare for taking the commercial driver's license exam. It includes practice tests.

Schauer, Donald D. *Careers in Trucking*. New York: The Rosen Publishing Group, Inc., 2000.
This book provides an overview of the many different careers in trucking. It also gives advice on how to get a job in the trucking industry.

BROCHURES

Careers in Trucking
http://www.ptdi.org/careers/index.htm
This brochure, sponsored by the Professional Truck Driver Institute, can be downloaded from the Web site listed above. It describes how to get into a career in truck driving and provides information on how to choose a truck driving school.

PERIODICALS

Roadstar
A magazine for professional truckers. Subscribe online, or call the phone number below.
http://www.roadstaronline.com
(800) 787-7808, ext. 14

8

MODEL, DEMONSTRATOR, AND PRODUCT PROMOTER

A model walks down a runway in Paris wearing the latest fashion designs. A demonstrator shows shoppers how to use a DVD player. A product promoter goes to a car show to unveil the new Porsche. What do these jobs have in common? All of the people doing these jobs are selling things, and all of them get to travel while doing so.

A fashion model strikes a pose to give buyers a good look at the outfit that she is showing. In addition to visiting major fashion centers in New York, London, and Paris, models often travel around the world for photo shoots.

Description

The job of a model is to convince people to buy things: clothes, makeup, jewelry, shoes, food, and many other types of products. Fashion models are photographed for ads in magazines, newspapers, or billboards. Many models appear in clothing catalogs. Others are filmed for television commercials. Some do live modeling, walking the runways at fashion shows or in department stores. The top models are known around the world and may have their own clothing line or fitness videos.

Some models specialize in one type of work. For instance, some model only specific parts of their body. Hand models, for example, advertise rings or nail polish. Some work as models for artists or sculptors.

Models can work all over the world and usually do not work for just one company. Their jobs usually last from a few hours to a few days. Most models do not have a regular schedule. They may work ten days in a row, but then have the next two weeks off. Sometimes their jobs are glamorous, like modeling at a fashion show in Milan, Italy, or posing for a swimsuit calendar in Hawaii. Other times they must stand in the cold while the photographer waits for the sun to come out from behind a cloud. They must be patient while stylists fix their hair and makeup.

Product promoters or demonstrators try to interest people in buying a certain product. To do that they go to stores, state fairs, car shows, and many other places to show their product and tell the public about it. Sometimes product promoters and demonstrators give out free samples or gifts to customers. Sometimes they even wear costumes or sign boards in public to advertise new products. Product promoters and demonstrators work for department stores, market research firms, or the company that makes the product that they are promoting.

As with models, product promoters and demonstrators usually do not have regular schedules. They may work nights and weekends at state fairs or trade shows all over the country. While they are working, they may be on duty for many hours and may have to stand or talk for long periods of time.

However, the chance to travel and the opportunity to meet lots of people make it worthwhile to many people who become product promoters or demonstrators.

Education and Training

Models don't need any special training to begin their career. However, becoming a model is not something that everyone can do. Models need to be attractive and physically fit. In general, fashion models need to be tall and thin.

Modeling schools are one way to get training and experience as a model. Going to a school is not always a requirement, though. Most modeling agencies give their models all the training they need, so paying for an expensive school isn't necessary. Getting an agent is an important first step to beginning a modeling career. Agents can help you to get work and advise you on your career. Check the For More Information section for books and Web sites that can tell you more about finding an agent.

To be a product promoter or demonstrator, you need a high school degree and good communication skills. Most product promoters get their training on the job. The stores or companies they work for teach them about the products that they will be selling. Demonstrators sometimes need special skills, such as cooking.

Being able to speak well and convince people to buy your product are the most important parts of the job of a

Models are often used to enhance the look of a product. They can have tremendous influence on the company's image.

product promoter or demonstrator. To prepare, it's a good idea to take public speaking courses or drama classes. These will help you to become comfortable speaking in front of groups. Voice or dance lessons can also be helpful.

Salary

Most demonstrators and product promoters earn between $7.71 and $13.51 per hour. Most models earn between $7 and $13.70. However, top models can earn much more. Some models also get clothes or other products in addition to their salary. According to the Bureau of Labor Statistics, models who work with agents usually have to pay their agents from 15 percent to 20 percent of their salary.

Outlook

The number of jobs for models, product promoters, and demonstrators is expected to grow in the coming years. More and more companies are finding that product promoters and demonstrators are very effective sales tools. There should be plenty of opportunities for jobs in that field. The Bureau of Labor Statistics predicts it will remain very competitive to get jobs in modeling.

FOR MORE INFORMATION

ORGANIZATIONS

American Marketing Association
250 S. Wacker Drive, Suite 200
Chicago, IL 60606
(312) 648-0536
Web site: http://www.marketingpower.com
The American Marketing Association has information on careers as product promoters and demonstrators. Their Web site has job listings.

The Models Guild
265 W. 14th Street, Suite 203
New York, NY 10011
(800) 864-4696
e-mail: models@opeiu.org
Web site: http://64.78.56.99/models/index.asp
The Models Guild is a union for models. The FYI section of their Web site tells you what kind of scams to watch out for.

WEB SITES

Learn More About Modeling
http://www.modelingadvice.com/learnmore.html
This site has an overview of modeling careers and has links to helpful books and videos.

ModelLaunch.com
http://www.modellaunch.com
This site is full of information for male models, including articles, tips, and information on agencies.

Modelresource.com
http://www.modelresource.com/home/main.htm
You'll find many resources for models on this site. There is information on schools, tips and techniques, and profiles of famous models.

SoYouWanna.com
http://www.soyouwanna.com/site/syws/model/model.html
SoYouWanna.com gives practical advice on many topics. The modeling section of the site tells you about the modeling industry and gives you advice on avoiding scams and getting started on your career.

Supermodelguide.com
http://www.supermodelguide.com
Designed by a former model, this informative site has tips, links to books and agencies, and articles on what it takes to be a model.

BOOKS

Esch, Natasha, with C. L. Walker. *The Wilhemina Guide to Modeling*. New York: Fireside Books, 1996.
This book has everything you need to know to get started in modeling. There are chapters on male modeling and modeling in other countries.

Gearheart, Susan Wood. *Opportunities in Modeling Careers*. Lincolnwood, IL: VGM Career Horizons, 1999.
You'll learn more about modeling agencies, how to get started on your career, and ideas for turning your modeling skills into future business opportunities.

Press, Debbie, and Skip Press. *Your Modeling Career: You Don't Have to Be a Superstar to Succeed*. New York: Allworth Press, 2000.
This book describes different types of modeling careers. It also has information about getting started in the modeling business.

Rose, Yvonne, and Tony Rose. *Is Modeling for You?: The Handbook and Guide for the Young Aspiring Black Model*. Los Angeles, CA: Amber Books, 1997.
This guide to getting into modeling has tips and information on agencies that specialize in African American models.

Steinberg, Margery. *Opportunities in Marketing Careers*. Lincolnwood, IL: VGM Career Horizons, 1999.
You can find information on product promoters and demonstrators, as well as other careers in marketing in this book.

PERIODICALS

Vogue
Conde Nast Publications
4 Times Square
New York, NY 10036
(212) 286-2860
http://www.vogue.com
This consumer-style magazine has information on fashion, makeup, and modeling.

PHOTO-JOURNALIST

A volcano erupts in Africa, and you are there. The winning goal is kicked through the posts at a World Cup soccer game in Brazil, and you are there. The president goes to Russia to visit the new prime minister, and you are there. As a photojournalist, you could cover any one of these stories. Your pictures could bring the world to readers of newspapers and magazines back home.

A photojournalist is caught in a stream of pepper spray as he tries to photograph police response to demonstrators in Washington, D.C. Nevertheless, he relentlessly tries to get "the best shot."

The life of a photojournalist is not an easy one. Photojournalists often work long hours and are usually not on a regular schedule. They might be awakened at 2:00 AM and told that they need to be in another country the next morning. Sometimes the job can be dangerous. It can often be uncomfortable lugging around heavy equipment or waiting outside in the rain for something to happen. But if you love to take photographs, have a good eye and a sense of business and adventure, and are ready to pick up and go at a moment's notice, photojournalism might be for you.

Description

Photojournalism is described in *Careers for Shutterbugs and Other Candid Types* as "reporting with a camera." Photojournalists tell a story with images.

Photojournalists cover many types of stories. Someone who works for a local newspaper may photograph car accidents or school plays. A photojournalist who works for a newsmagazine such as *Newsweek* might cover peace talks in the Middle East or a presidential election. Sports photographers might shoot the NBA basketball season from start to finish, in cities all over the country.

As a photojournalist you may work for one publication or agency, or you can choose to be a freelancer. This means that you would work for many different companies or publications. If you really like to travel, being a freelance photojournalist may be the right option for you.

Another way to be guaranteed some travel time is to work for a major publication such as *Time* magazine, which could send you all over the world to cover stories. Photojournalists employed by sports photo agencies also cover a lot of ground. As a sports photographer covering professional baseball, for example, your typical day might consist of getting up early to travel to the field and check your equipment. In the afternoon you would get your cameras set up in the ballpark. You might socialize with the other reporters or even the players. During

Nature photojournalists travel all over the world to shoot some of Earth's most breathtaking views. In doing so, they often come across scenes and events that most people will never see—except, perhaps, in print.

the game you would be busy capturing the action on the field. Most of the real work happens after the game. You would quickly check the shots you got during the game and pick the best ones. If you worked for a newspaper you would rush to send the pictures (digital cameras are making this increasingly faster) to the newsroom. They need to get the photos so that they can get them printed in the morning edition.

Education and Training

There are many ways to get started in photojournalism. You can work as an assistant to a professional photographer.

Working at a photo lab or photo studio is another way to gain experience. A summer job or internship at a local newspaper or magazine can really teach you what the job is like.

It's also important to gain experience with digital cameras, scanners, and picture editing software. Although photojournalists will probably continue to use film cameras, all of them need to know how to work with computers. Take any photography classes your school offers, or investigate local community programs. Joining the photo staff of your school yearbook or newspaper is also a good place to start.

Salary

The Bureau of Labor Statistics lists salaries for photojournalists ranging from about $13,000 to more than $46,000 per year. They mention that freelance photographers generally earn less than photographers who work full-time for a newspaper or magazine.

Outlook

According to *The Best Jobs for the 21st Century, Third Edition*, average growth is predicted for photojournalists. However, there is a growing need for digital images for online versions of newspapers and magazines. As a result there may be an increase in the demand for photographers for news services.

Profile

INTERVIEW WITH ROBIN SHOTOLA

Robin Shotola has worked as a photojournalist at newspapers around the Northeast. She has also worked as a wedding photographer.

WHAT DO YOU LIKE BEST ABOUT PHOTOJOURNALISM?

Being outside experiencing things and meeting people every day is one of the best things about the job. The fact that it is not a 9-to-5 office job is good if you are the type of person who can't be cooped up all day.

WHAT DO YOU LIKE LEAST ABOUT PHOTOJOURNALISM?

When you are covering news stories you often have to photograph unpleasant things like fires or accidents. It's tough to see the bad things that happen to good people.

WHAT ADVICE WOULD YOU GIVE SOMEONE WHO WANTED TO GET INTO PHOTOJOURNALISM?

The thing that will get you a job is the pictures that you have to show. So the most important thing to do is to just start taking photos. You learn by doing, and you find out what makes a good picture.

Take whatever opportunity you can get. A lot of places need photographs, and small publications like local newspapers are a good place to start. Call the photo editor and offer to shoot for free. This will expose you to a wide range of assignments, and it will get your photographs published.

FOR MORE INFORMATION

ORGANIZATIONS

The American Society of Media Photographers, Inc. (ASMP)
150 North Second Street
Philadelphia, PA 19106
(215) 451-2767
Web site: http://www.asmp.org
ASMP provides information to photographers whose work appears in any kind of publication.

National Press Photographers Association (NPPA)
3200 Croasdaile Drive, Suite 360
Durham, NC 27705
(919) 383-7246
Web site: http://www.nppa.org
NPPA is a great resource for internships and general information about photojournalism. They also sponsor workshops.

Professional Photographers of America, Inc.
229 Peachtree Street NE, Suite 2200
Atlanta, GA 30303
(404) 522-8600
e-mail: csc@ppa.com
Web site: http://www.ppa.com
PPA has information on the business side of photography, as well as the creative side.

WEB SITES

Apogee Photo
http://www.apogeephoto.com
This online magazine has articles, contests, and a section for young photographers.

The Digital Filmmaker
http://digitalfilmmaker.net
Digital Filmmaker focuses on telling stories in pictures. There are links to other photojournalism sites, and a discussion group for photo-journalists with ideas on getting into photojournalism.

Fotofile.com
http://www.fotophile.com
In addition to a bookstore and gallery, this site features links to hundreds of photography-related Web sites.

PDN Online
http://www.pdn-pix.com
This is the online version of *Photo District News* magazine. It features news, articles, and information on new products.

BOOKS

Farr, J. Michael. *America's Top Jobs for People without a Four-Year Degree.* Fifth ed. Indianapolis, IN: JIST Works, Inc., 2001.
This book has information on careers in photography, as well as other careers that do not require college.

Horton, Brian. *Associated Press Guide to Photojournalism.* Second ed. New York: McGraw-Hill Professional, 2001.
Different types of photojournalism, techniques for taking good photographs, and interviews with photojournalists are highlighted in this book.

Kobre, Kenneth. *Photojournalism: The Professional's Approach.* Woburn, MA: Focal Press, 2000.
This textbook covers all aspects of photojournalism. It includes interviews with photojournalists and tips and techniques for taking great photographs.

McLean, Cheryl. *Careers for Shutterbugs and Other Candid Types.*
Lincolnwood, IL: VGM Career Horizons, 1995.
This book provides a good overview of different types of jobs in photojournalism.

PERIODICALS

Photo District News
To get a special student rate, orders must be sent to:
Photo District News
P.O. Box 1983
Marion, OH 43306-2083
Web site: http://www.pdn-pix.com/subscribe
Photo District News contains articles and information for professional photographers.

10

SURVEYING TECHNICIAN

Have you ever seen a worker standing in a field looking through a small instrument perched on a tripod? Did you wonder what that worker was doing? He or she was probably a surveying technician collecting on-site information that will later be used by a surveyor. Surveyors set official boundaries for land, air, and water. They describe land for legal purposes, measure construction sites, and even set air space for airports.

Surveying technicians can also work on more unusual projects—such as measuring recently discovered tombs in Egypt, or meteor craters in Mexico. Surveying technicians even helped workers at Ground Zero, the recovery site of the World Trade Center towers in New York City. They used their equipment to monitor the buildings and give warnings about any structures that were in danger of falling. They also helped the workers find appropriate locations to set up cranes.

Description

Surveying technicians work on teams called survey parties. They operate the equipment that measures the area that they are surveying. They take detailed notes, make sketches of the area, and record all the data into a computer.

Much of a surveying technician's day is spent outside, and often he or she gets to travel. Sometimes surveying technicians drive to the site to be surveyed, but sometimes they need to travel a greater distance to the site. Occasionally they will temporarily move to the survey site.

Being a surveying technician can be physically demanding. Surveying technicians often have to stand for long periods of time or walk great distances. There is a lot of heavy equipment to be carried, and they may be outside in all types of weather.

Who Works on a Surveying Party?

A land survey party collects information the surveyor needs from a particular location. There are usually four to eight people in the party. Here are some of the party's members:

Party chief (land surveyor or senior survey technician): leads the group and makes sure measurements are accurate

Surveying technician: helps the party chief, operates equipment, and takes notes

Assistant: helps operate equipment

Helper: carries equipment, clears the land to make it easier to set up the equipment, sets up traffic warnings

Surveying technicians usually work a regular workweek, although they may work longer hours in the summer.

After working for several years, a surveying technician usually becomes a senior surveying technician. Then he or she can take exams to become licensed as a surveyor.

Education and Training

On-the-job training is usually the best way for surveying technicians to get experience. A surveying technician can

Because it is their job to measure construction and disaster sites, land surveyors have a unique perspective of the changes an area goes through.

A surveyor's job could bring him or her deep underground, forcing the surveyor to work under difficult conditions.

get started working as an apprentice to a surveying team. Since surveying teams often have more work during warmer months, they may hire high school students for the summer.

There are vocational schools that offer one-, two-, or three-year programs in surveying or surveying engineering technology. If you earn an associate's degree from a vocational school you can often start working at a higher salary level than if you had started working straight from high school.

To prepare for a career as a surveying technician, there are several courses that you can take in high school that will give you a good background. Math classes such as algebra, geometry, and trigonometry are recommended. Computer science classes will help you to prepare for working with the equipment that surveyors use. Classes in drafting or mechanical drawing will help you to learn technical drawing skills.

Surveying technicians are employed by architects and engineers or by construction companies. State and local governments and government agencies such as the Forest Service or the U.S. Geological Survey also hire surveying technicians.

Land, Air, and Water

Surveys aren't just done on land. Here are some of the techniques surveyors use to map on land, in the air, and underwater. Land surveying technicians use tools such as a global positioning system (GPS), which uses radio signals from satellites to give precise locations. Surveying can be done from the air by attaching a camera to the bottom of a plane. The plane flies over the area being surveyed and takes many pictures. The pictures are then put together with a computer to produce an accurate image. Surveys can also be done underwater using sonar.

Salary

According to the Bureau of Labor Statistics, most surveying technicians earn between $10.46 and $17.81 per hour. Surveying technicians who work for local, state, or federal governments earn more than technicians who work for engineering or architectural firms. Surveying technicians who work for the federal government earn an average salary of $34,623.

Outlook

Jobs for surveying technicians are expected to increase faster than average, according to the Bureau of Labor Statistics. An increase in construction of schools, offices, and other buildings is expected. This will lead to more jobs for surveyors to help lay out streets and sites for buildings. Surveying technicians will also help measure land for environmentally protected areas.

FOR MORE INFORMATION

ORGANIZATIONS

American Congress on Surveying and Mapping (ACSM)
6 Montgomery Village Avenue, Suite 403
Gaithersburg, MD 20879

(240) 632-9716 ext. 106
Web site: http://www.acsm.net
ACSM is an educational organization to which many surveyors belong.

Canadian Council of Land Surveyors (CCLS)

1390 Prince of Wales Drive, Suite 400
Ottawa, Ontario, Canada K2C 3N6
(800) 241-7200
Web site: http://www.ccls-ccag.ca/index.html
CCLS is a Canadian professional organization for surveyors.

The National Council of Examiners for Engineering and Surveying (NCEES)

280 Seneca Creek Road
Clemson, SC 29633-1686
(800) 250-3196
Web site: http://www.ncees.org
The NCEES tests and licenses surveyors.

National Society of Professional Surveyors, Inc. (NSPS)

5410 Grosvenor Lane, Suite 100
Bethesda, MD 20814
(301) 493-0200
Web site: http://www.acsm.net/nsps/index.html
This branch of ACSM is an organization for professional surveyors.

WEB SITES

LandSurveyors.com

http://www.bls.gov/k12/html/gym_005.htm
LandSurveyors.com has great resources for surveyors. The site also offers job postings at various levels.

Land Surveyor Reference Page

http://www.lsrp.com
Featuring links to many other Web sites for surveyors, this site also has job postings and discussion rooms.

SurveyCareers.com
http://www.surveycareers.com
Listings for surveying jobs are posted on this site. There are also links to educational resources.

Trimble.com
http://www.trimble.com/gps/
Use this tutorial to learn more about global positioning systems (GPS).

Virtual Museum of Surveying
http://www.surveyhistory.org/
Take a tour of surveying equipment and get other information on surveying on this site.

BOOKS

Farr, J. Michael. *America's Top Jobs for People without a Four-Year Degree.* Fifth ed. Indianapolis, IN: JIST Works, Inc., 2001.
This book has a good general overview of surveying, as well as descriptions of other careers that do not require college.

Wolf, Paul R., and Charles D. Ghilani. *Elementary Surveying: An Introduction to Geomatics.* Tenth ed. Upper Saddle River, NJ: Prentice-Hall, Inc., 2001.
This is a textbook on surveying basics.

PERIODICALS

Professional Surveyor
Professional Surveyors Publishing Co., Inc.
100 Tuscanny Drive
Suite B1
Frederick, MD 21702
(301) 682-6101
Web site: http://www.profsurv.com
Professional Surveyor has information on surveying, as well as job listings and information on education and equipment.

11

CRUISE SHIP ENTERTAINER

Have you ever dreamed of living the glamorous life of a dancer or singer? What if you got to see the world while pursuing your dream of being an entertainer? That is exactly what cruise ship entertainers do. They get paid to do what they love while they live and eat for free on a cruise ship.

A cruise ship dance instructor teaches steps to a group of passengers.

Description

If you have a talent for singing, music, dancing, comedy, or even juggling, and you love to travel, a job as an entertainer on a cruise ship might be for you. There are many different kinds of jobs for entertainers on cruise ships. Most nights there is a large show featuring dancers, singers, and musicians. There are also solo acts such as those by magicians or comedians. Musicians can be part of an orchestra that plays while guests dance. They can also be in smaller bands that play on deck during an activity.

Many entertainers take part in the big shows that are often the highlight of the evening for cruise passengers. These shows also need costume designers, lighting technicians, choreographers, and producers.

Entertainers on cruise ships work hard, but they also have free time to enjoy the ship. The big shows are late in the evening, and, except for a rehearsal in the afternoon, entertainers can go ashore or relax on the ship most of the day.

In addition to their regular shows, entertainers sometimes have other duties. They may greet passengers, help out with activities and games, or perform at deck parties. Entertainers are often required to talk with passengers, so they need to be friendly and outgoing.

If you're an entertainer who loves to travel but you're not sure that life on a cruise ship is for you, consider working at a resort. Many resorts all over the world have shows each night to entertain their guests. The shows may feature singers, dancers, or musicians. Often musicians are also hired to play at the pool or beach to entertain the guests during the day.

Education and Training

Whether you're a musician, juggler, or dancer, the most important thing to do is practice your skill. Perform in plays, musicals, or talent shows. Practice will help you to develop

People Who Can Help You Get a Job with a Cruise Line

There are several types of people who can be helpful when it comes time to find a job. A **manager** can give you advice on what to wear and what kind of act to do. He or she can also help you get work with an agency. **Agencies** often work closely with cruise lines and help ships hire entertainers. A **producer** puts shows together, hiring entertainers as well as costume designers, and sound and light people. The producer then sells the whole show to a cruise line. See the For More Information section for agency and producer contact information.

your talent. It will also help you to gain confidence. In *How to Get a Job with a Cruise Line*, Pam Jaye, a dancer on a cruise ship, says that cruise ships are "looking for confidence. Find one thing you're good at and use this to build your self-confidence."

While you're working on your skill, you can also research cruise ships. Find out what cruise lines specialize in. You can also research agencies that hire entertainers for cruise lines. Once you've done your research and your skills

A couple enjoys the music of a mariachi band on a luxury cruise. Cruise directors are always on the lookout for fresh talent to add flair to the ship's entertainment.

are ready to be put to the test, make a videotape to show off your talent. Keep the tape short, and make sure it looks professional. Most cruise ship entertainers got their jobs by sending videotapes or auditioning in person. See the sidebar on the preceding page to find out more about who can help you get a job on a cruise ship.

Salary

Globalshipservices.com lists salaries for musicians at between $1,600 and $2,150 per month. Singers and dancers

Other Jobs on a Cruise Ship

Some cruise ships are like small cities, with hundreds of workers. Here are just a few of the jobs that need to be filled on a cruise ship: bartender, barber/hairdresser, casino worker, chef, electrician, fitness instructor, massage therapist, navigation officer, nurse, photographer, psychic, scuba/snorkeling instructor, youth counselor.

make between $1,600 and $2,800 per month. Employees of cruise ships get all their expenses paid. They also have free medical care and a clothing allowance.

Outlook

Cruise ships are a very popular vacation mode, and experts expect the industry to continue growing. This means more passengers will need to be entertained in the coming years. Talented entertainers should have plenty of opportunities to find work on the high seas.

FOR MORE INFORMATION

ORGANIZATIONS

Agencies and Production Companies

Bramson Entertainment Bureau
630 Ninth Avenue, Suite 203
New York, NY 10036
(212) 265-3500
Web site: http://www.bramson.com/general.html
Bramson is one of the top employment agencies for cruise ship entertainers.

Cruise Lines International Association (CLIA)

500 Fifth Avenue, Suite 1407
New York, New York 10110
(212) 921-0066
e-mail: info@cruising.org
Web site: http://www.cruising.org
CLIA is the official organization of the cruise industry. They work with cruise lines and travel agents.

International Council of Cruise Lines (ICCL)

2111 Wilson Boulevard, 8th Floor
Arlington, VA 22201
(800) 595-9338
e-mail: info@iccl.org
Web site: http://www.iccl.org
The ICCL provides information on its members, which include many of the major cruise lines. They also do research on the cruise industry.

Jean Ann Ryan Productions, Inc.
308 SE 14th Street
Fort Lauderdale, FL 33316
(954) 523-6399
e-mail: jarjobs@aol.com
Web site: http://www.jeanannryanproductions.com
This company produces shows for cruise ships and corporate events.

Proship Entertainment
5253 Decarie Boulevard, Suite 308
Montreal, Quebec, Canada   H3W 3C2
(514) 485-8823
e-mail: info@proship.com
Web site: http://www.Proship.com
Based in Canada, this agency helps musicians and entertainers get jobs on cruise ships.

WEB SITES

CoolWorks.com
http://www.coolworks.com
Check the Jobs on Water section for links to cruise ship jobs.

Cruise Ship Database
http://www.jcoston.bizland.com/cruisedbfr.html
This database provides complete address information for cruise ship companies based in the United States and abroad.

JobMonkey.com
http://www.jobmonkey.com/cruise
This site has excellent information about getting into the cruise industry and has job postings.

ResortJobs.com
http://www.resortjobs.com/do/where
This site features links to cruise and resort jobs worldwide. Check the Resources section for links to internship and summer job opportunities.

BOOKS

Eberts, Marjorie, Linda Brothers, and Ann Gisler. *Careers in Travel, Tourism, and Hospitality*. Lincolnwood, IL: VGM Career Horizons, 1997. An overview of careers in the cruise industry is included in this book about travel careers.

Goldberg, Jan. *Opportunities in Entertainment Careers.* Lincolnwood, IL: VGM Career Horizons, 1999.
This is a general guide to careers in acting, music, dance, and related occupations.

Marin, Richard B. *Cruise Ship Jobs: The Insiders Guide to Finding and Getting Jobs on Cruise Ships Around the World*. Coconut Creek, FL: Portofino Publications, 1998.
You can find detailed information on being a cruise ship entertainer in this book. It also contains answers to many common questions about life on cruise ships.

Miller, Mary Fallon. *How to Get a Job with a Cruise Line.* Fourth ed. St. Petersburg, FL: Ticket to Adventure, Inc., 1997.
This book contains practical information on how to get a job on a cruise ship. It also features profiles of people who have held cruise ship jobs.

PERIODICALS

Cruise Travel
http://www.cruisetravelmag.com
Read this magazine to get general information on cruises.

Travel Weekly
(800) 360-0015
e-mail: twcrossroads@cahners.com
Web site: http://www.twcrossroads.com
Travel Weekly is a good magazine to read to learn about the travel industry.

TOUR GUIDE

Have you always wanted to see the world, but weren't sure you would be able to afford it? One solution to that problem is to become a tour guide. Being a tour guide is a "unique way to see the world, and get paid to do it," writes Marc Mancini in his book *Conducting Tours: A Practical Guide.*

Description

Tour guides are sometimes called tour managers or tour escorts. They may meet their group at the airport or travel with them to their destination. They help everyone in the group get their luggage or go through customs. The tour guide then travels with the group, making sure the group gets where it's supposed to be—on time and in one piece.

Tour guides are on duty twenty-four hours a day seven days a week when they're on a tour. They are usually the first ones to wake up and the last ones to go to sleep. A tour guide double-checks everything before the tour, and keeps double-checking all the arrangements during the tour.

Being a tour guide can be stressful. Tour guides put in long days, and even if they are tired they have to solve any problems that come up along the way, such as lost suitcases and stolen wallets. One of the most important jobs that a tour guide has is making sure that all the customers on the tour are having a great time. Tour guides are paid to make sure that things go smoothly and to help customers get what they need.

Not all tour guides travel with one particular group. Some tour guides work in a specific city and will give driving or walking tours of that city. These types of guides need to know a lot about a particular location, and must want to share their love of that location with others. Other guides have a specialized

What Does It Take to Be a Good Tour Guide?

Heidi Friederich, a tour guide for more than twenty years, has led trips to France, Germany, the Netherlands, Ireland, and many cities in the United States and Canada.

"To be a good tour guide you need to be organized and flexible. Unexpected things always seem to happen and you must be able to react immediately and solve the problem at once. You also need a good sense of humor so that you can laugh at these disasters later!

"You also need to love being with people for an extended time; often you are together with your group all day and evening. It is tiring but very rewarding when you see how much people appreciate all that you have done for them to make their trip enjoyable."

knowledge of a country, or have a skill that helps them lead an unusual type of trip, such as a safari. "Step-on" guides are hired by a tour company to give a talk or a tour to a visiting group. These guides might get on a tour bus and give a lecture as the bus drives to various locations around a city.

Tour guides might lead tours for months at a time, but then have a month or two off to rest up or travel on their

A tour guide listens to a tourist's question during a ferry ride on the Mekong Delta in Vietnam. Guides must be prepared to answer questions about the locations they visit.

own. Tour guides sometimes get to travel to a new place for free to check it out and become familiar with it before leading a group there.

Education and Training

Most tour guides will tell you that your work experience is much more important than going to school to be a guide. There are some schools that offer courses in tour management that last from one month to one year. See the For More Information section for some schools that offer these programs.

A tour guide shares facts about the Liberty Bell during a tour of Independence National Historical Park in Philadelphia, Pennsylvania. The tour also includes Independence Hall and the site of Ben Franklin's house.

Tour guides need to be organized, responsible, and ready to deal with any situation. Helping to plan school trips or managing a sports team at your high school might help you to develop those skills. You also need good customer service skills. Working as a guide in a local museum, or working in a hotel or restaurant, will help you to polish your people skills. It would also help to study a foreign language or two, to learn as much history as possible, and to take a public speaking class.

When you are ready to become a tour guide, many tour companies will train you by sending you on tours with an experienced guide. You assist the guide and learn about the place you are visiting. Watch the guide closely to see how he or she handles the people on the tour, or handles problems that come up. Soon you will be ready to lead a tour on your own.

Salary

The amount of money a tour guide can make varies greatly. Some tour guides are paid a regular salary even when they are not out leading a tour. Other tour guides lead tours only during one particular season and make less money as a result.

In addition to the money they are paid for leading a tour, tour guides often get tips from their customers. Other benefits are that all their expenses are paid while they are leading the tour. Sometimes guides get to travel for free when they go to potential new tour sites.

Outlook

Group travel is growing faster than other types of travel. This means that the need for tour guides will probably increase. The Bureau of Labor Statistics expects jobs for tour guides to grow over the next ten years.

FOR MORE INFORMATION

ORGANIZATIONS

American Society of Travel Agents (ASTA)
1101 King Street, Suite 200
Alexandria, VA 22314
(703) 739-2782
Web site: http://www.astanet.com
ASTA is the leading organization for travel professionals. Check the Education/Careers section of its Web site to get information on travel schools.

National Tour Association (NTA)
120 Kentucky Avenue
Lexington, KY 40502
(859) 226-4444
Web site: http://www.ntaonline.com
The NTA has information on companies that run tours, news about the tour industry, and resources for tour guides.

United States Tour Operators Association (USTOA)
275 Madison Avenue, Suite 2014
New York, NY 10016
(212) 599-6599
e-mail: information@ustoa.com
Web site: http://www.ustoa.com
Reputable tour operators belong to this association. You can search their Web site for tour companies that belong to USTOA.

SCHOOLS

International Guide Academy (IGA)

P.O. Box 19649
Boulder, CO 80308-2649
(303) 530-3420
Web site: http://www.igaonline.com/home.html
IGA offers a four-week course, four times a year. They train and certify professional international tour managers and tour guides.

International Tour Management Institute, Inc.

625 Market Street, Suite 810
San Francisco, CA 94105
(800) 442-4864
Web site: http://www.itmitourtraining.com
This school trains professional tour directors and guides. They have three locations in the United States.

WEB SITES

JobMonkey.com

http://www.jobmonkey.com/landtours
Along with a great overview of being a tour guide, this site has job listings for tour guides.

BOOKS

Crisfield, Deborah. *Now Hiring: Travel*. New York: Crestwood House, 1994.
This book has a chapter on tour guides, as well as information about other travel careers.

Hawks, John K. *Career Opportunities in Travel and Tourism*. New York: Facts On File, Inc., 1995.
Offering a chapter on how to become a tour guide, this book also has general information on travel careers.

Mancini, Marc. *Conducting Tours: A Practical Guide.* Third Edition. Albany, NY: Delmar Publishers, 2000.
This textbook has profiles of tour guides and activities to help you get a feel for what tour guiding is like.

PERIODICALS

National Geographic Traveler
http://www.nationalgeographic.com/traveler
Learn about exciting places all over the world with the stories and pictures in this magazine.

VIDEOS

An Introduction to Tour Management
This video, produced by the International Tour Management Institute, can help you decide if being a tour guide is for you. To order call (800) 442-4864 or visit their web site at http://www.itmitourtraining.com/html/video.html

13

TRAIN CONDUCTOR

Have you ever wanted to be the person shouting "All aboard!" when a train is leaving the station? If you'd like to see the country while riding the rails, a job as a train conductor might be the right one for you.

Description

Conductors can work on two types of trains: passenger or freight.

Train conductors assist a passenger as she steps off a train in Cape Cod, Massachusetts. Passengers expect train conductors to be helpful with such information as directions to main locations or where to find a taxi.

Freight trains carry all kinds of cargo. Conductors who work on them have to keep track of the cargo. They have to know where the cargo is being dropped off and where the train has to pick up more.

Passenger conductors work on trains that carry people. Their job is to take tickets, hand out schedules, help passengers, and announce train stops. On some passenger trains, there are assistant conductors who help collect tickets and help passengers with their baggage.

Being a freight conductor is hard work. Since freight conductors spend a lot of their time outside, they must be able to handle different weather and climate conditions. It may be sizzling hot outside but icy cold inside the cars. Freight conductors sometimes help to hook and unhook the cargo cars, and climbing on and off the cars can sometimes be dangerous. Freight trains do not run on regular schedules. Freight conductors often get called to work on short notice. Because freight trains travel long distances, freight conductors might be away from home for many nights in a row.

Passenger trains have a more regular schedule, so passenger conductors usually know when they will be scheduled to work. But like freight conductors, passenger conductors often have to work nights, weekends, and holidays.

Education and Training

Conductors need a high school degree or GED. Most railroads will provide training, offering classes and on-the-job experience. Conductors usually start as brake operators and move up to the position of conductor when there is an opening. When they first start they usually do not have a regular schedule. Instead they fill in for other conductors who are out sick or on vacation. Eventually they get a regular schedule.

You do not need any special skills to be a conductor, although you do need to be in good health and have good

Baby on the Board

When a conductor begins working for a railroad, he or she becomes the "baby on the board." He or she is the person with the least number of years working for the railroad and has to "do every kind of railroad work in every location," says Cindy Angelos, a Milwaukee Road conductor profiled in *Railroad Voices*. The baby on the board goes wherever there is a shortage and may have to drive far from home every day. Sometimes they are "loaned" to another railroad for a while. Some railroad workers are called "boomers" and they go anywhere in the country they can find work.

eyesight. If you want to be a conductor on a passenger train you will need good people skills, so it helps to have some customer service experience.

Salary

Most freight conductors earn about $53,500 and passenger conductors earn about $68,000, according to the National Railroad Labor Conference. Nearly all conductors belong to unions and receive competitive salaries and good benefits. They also get paid well for working overtime.

An Amtrak conductor gives an all clear signal to the head conductor before the train departs Boston's South Station for Portland, Maine. Working as a train conductor is a great way to tour the country.

Outlook

Jobs for conductors may decline slightly in the coming years. Railroads may be used more to transport freight, but newer trains need fewer people to operate them. There may be an increased need for streetcar and subway operators because more cities are adding public transportation, according to the Bureau of Labor Statistics.

FOR MORE INFORMATION

ORGANIZATIONS

American Public Transportation Association (APTA)
1666 K Street NW, Suite 1100
Washington, DC 20006
(202) 496-4800
Web site: http://www.apta.com
To learn more about public transportation in the United States and Canada, check the APTA Web site. They also have links to schools in the United States and other countries.

Association of American Railroads (AAR)
American Railroads Building
50 F Street NW
Washington, DC 20001
(202) 639-2100
Web site: http://www.aar.org
The AAR works to improve safety on all North American railroads.

Federal Railroad Administration (FRA)
1120 Vermont Avenue NW
Washington, DC 20590
Web site: http://www.fra.dot.gov/site/index.htm
The FRA regulates railroads and is part of the U.S. Department of Transportation. Be sure to check the Learning Depot page on their Web site for information on railroad careers.

Railway Association of Canada (RAC)
99 Bank Street, Suite 1401
Ottawa, Ontario, Canada K1P 6B9

(613) 567-8591
e-mail: rac@railcan.ca
Web site: http://www.railcan.ca/en/welcome/default.htm
The RAC is an association of Canadian railroads. Check the Careers and Institute of Railway Technology section of their Web site for information on schools.

United Transportation Union (UTU)
14600 Detroit Avenue
Cleveland, OH 44107-4250
Web site: http://www.utu.org
UTU is the union to which most railway workers belong. They have information on regulations and their Web site has links to all major railroads in the United States and Canada.

SCHOOLS
The National Academy of Railroad Sciences
Johnson City Community College
12345 College Boulevard
Overland Park, KS 66210
(913) 469-8500
This community college can train you for a railroad job. Their Web site has information on their school and other schools in the United States.

Wisconsin and Southern Railroad Company
5300 North 33rd Street
Milwaukee, WI 53209
(414) 438-8820
http://www.wsorrailroad.com
This railroad company offers training for freight railroad work. Their Web site also has job listings.

WEB SITES

WhoHasJobs.com
http://www.whohasjobs.com/field/019/index.htm
This site has many listings for railway jobs, as well as other jobs in transportation.

BOOKS

Farr, J. Michael. *America's Top Jobs for People without a Four-Year Degree.* Fifth ed. Indianapolis, IN: JIST Works, Inc., 2001.
This book gives a good overview of railroad careers and has information on other careers that don't require a college degree.

Krannich, Ronald, and Caryl Rae Krannich. *Jobs for People Who Love to Travel: Opportunities at Home and Abroad.* Third ed. Manassas Park, VA: Impact Publications, 1999.
A brief overview of jobs with a railroad can be found in this book on travel careers.

Loomis, Jim. *All Aboard!: The Complete North American Train Travel Guide.* Second ed. Roseville, CA: Prima Publishing, 1998.
With information on people who work on a train as well as everything you need to know to plan a train trip in North America, this is a great book for first-time train travelers.

Niemann, Linda. *Railroad Voices.* Stanford, CA: Stanford University Press, 1998.
This book has stories and pictures of life working for a railroad.

PERIODICALS

Trains
(888) 350-2413
e-mail: customerservice@trains.com
Web site: http://www.trains.com
This magazine and its online version have information on the railroad industry, model trains, and rail travel.

14

TRAVEL AGENT

Do you like learning about far-away places as much as you like visiting them? If you also like helping people and planning trips, being a travel agent might be a good career choice. Travel agents give people advice on where to go, where to stay, and how to get there.

A travel agent shows a couple a destination on the map. Many tourist boards invite travel agents on free trips to give them an idea of the vacation they are selling.

Description

A travel agent may help someone book a flight or get a rental car for a trip to Disney World. Or he or she may help a traveler book a round-the-world cruise. These agents specialize in leisure (vacation) travel. Other agents specialize in travel for business people. This is called corporate travel. These agents help business people make reservations or plan meetings.

Travel agents may specialize in a particular type of travel. Some may help customers book cruises. Others work on-site for a large company or university, helping them book travel for their employees or students.

If you love to travel, you'll be happy to hear that the best part of the job for most travel agents is that they often get to travel for free. They go on familiarization or "fam" trips that help them get to know a new country, a new hotel, or a new cruise line. Usually these trips are paid by airlines, hotels, or cruise lines. These companies hope that if the travel agent enjoys the trip, he or she will recommend them to their clients. Although these trips are not really vacations, they are a good opportunity to see new places all over the world.

Education and Training

There are many ways to get started as a travel agent. There are schools that offer full-time or night and weekend courses for people who want to become travel agents. These classes are usually from six to eighteen weeks long.

One way to get started is to work in a travel agency doing office work, such as filing and photocopying, and helping to plan simple trips. Once you have some experience in the office, you can begin planning more complex trips. Some agencies will hire high school students to work afternoons or weekends.

Travel agents are trained on the special computer systems used by the airlines, but it is a good idea to practice using computers beforehand. Learning general business and office skills is also helpful.

John Riel, Corporate Travel Agent

"One summer I spent three weeks traveling around Europe on the train. It was the first time I had traveled, and I loved it. I wasn't sure what I wanted to do for a career, but I did know I wanted to travel more. Looking through the paper one day I saw an ad for a travel school that offered a three-month course.

"I really enjoyed the class and at the end of three months got a job working in leisure travel. It involved booking everything from plane, to car, to train, to cruise reservations. The office I worked in was extremely busy, but I learned a lot very fast because of it. I worked in leisure travel for five years and now have worked in corporate travel for the last seven years. Corporate travel involves setting up client business trips. I enjoy this much more than leisure because most of the clients travel often and know what they want. But because of this, they can be very demanding. Business travel also changes constantly. Meetings get

Continued on next page

Travel agents often go on trips to help them plan vacations for others. Vacationers like to get a firsthand description of the features of the resorts they intend to visit.

changed or cancelled and plans must be continuously revised. Anyone going into this field must be flexible.

"The thing I like best about being a travel agent is the opportunity to travel and learn about different places and cultures. I have been able to travel to many places that I probably would not have gone to other- wise. My favorite trips have been to Kenya/Tanzania on safari and to Peru to Machu Picchu."

A tourist and a guide observe wildlife in Masai Mara in Kenya, Africa.

Learning about other countries can also help a travel agent in his or her job. John Riel, a corporate travel agent, says that being a travel agent "is a constant learning process [because] it would be impossible to know every destination in the world. However, one thing a high school student could do to prepare for the job would be to study geography. Having that knowledge is a huge help."

One of the most important things a travel agent needs to be able to do is listen. It is essential to understand what the client really wants. If the travel agent succeeds in making customers happy, they will come back again.

Salary

The Bureau of Labor Statistics says that most travel agents earn between $19,890 and $31,820 per year. Travel agents employed by a travel company receive benefits and a regular salary. Agents who own their own companies might not be able to depend on a regular salary or benefits. Small companies make most of their money from commissions that they receive from airlines, cruise lines, and hotels.

Outlook

The number of travel agents is expected to grow over the next ten years, according to the Bureau of Labor Statistics. The number of people traveling will probably increase, although not everyone will use a travel agent. Many people are now using the Internet to make their own travel plans.

FOR MORE INFORMATION

ORGANIZATIONS

Alliance of Canadian Travel Associations (ACTA)
130 Albert Street, Suite 1705
Ottawa, Ontario, Canada K1P 5G4
(613) 237-3657
Web site: http://www.acta.ca
This is an association to which many Canadian travel agents belong.

American Society of Travel Agents (ASTA)
1101 King Street, Suite 200
Alexandria, VA 22314
(703) 739-2782
Web site: http://www.astanet.com
ASTA is the leading organization for travel professionals. Check the Education/Careers section of its Web site to get information on travel schools.

Institute of Certified Travel Agents (ICTA)
148 Linden Street
Wellesley, MA 02482
(800) 542-4282
Web site: http://www.icta.com
ICTA trains and certifies travel professionals. Their Web site can help you find schools near you and can help you plan your travel career.

International Airlines Travel Agent Network (IATAN)
300 Garden City Plaza, Suite 342
Garden City, NY 11530-3302
(516) 663-6000
e-mail: info@iatan.org
Web site: http://www.iatan.org/index.htm
IATAN has many services travel agents can use. Check their Web site for travel videos and information on training.

WEB SITES

CNN.com Travel
http://www.cnn.com/TRAVEL
CNN has stories about travel to foreign countries, maps, and information about the travel industry.

National Geographic
http://www.nationalgeographic.com/siteindex/index.html#top
Check out the Maps and Geography section or the Travel section of this site for great resources.

TravelChannel.com
http://travel.discovery.com
The Travel Channel features stories on travel to locations all over the world. Their Web site has information on destinations, a free newsletter, and a store where you can buy travel videos.

SCHOOLS

Travel Agent University
Web site: http://www.tauniv.com
Sponsored by *Travel Agent* magazine, this online school offers classes you can take from home.

Travel Education Center (TEC)
Web site: http://www.traveleducation.com/Welcome.html
TEC is an online travel career program. They offer a sixteen-week course that can be taken from your home computer.

BOOKS

Eberts, Marjorie, Linda Brothers, and Ann Gisler. *Careers in Travel, Tourism, and Hospitality.* Lincolnwood, IL: VGM Career Horizons, 1997. An overview of what a travel agent does is included in this book about travel careers.

Farr, J. Michael. *America's Top Jobs for People without a Four-Year Degree.* Fifth ed. Indianapolis, IN: JIST Works, Inc., 2001. This book provides a general overview of what a travel agent does.

Krannich, Ronald, and Caryl Rae Krannich. *Jobs for People Who Love to Travel: Opportunities at Home and Abroad.* Third ed. Manassas Park, VA: Impact Publications, 1999. This book provides general information on a career as a travel agent.

PERIODICALS

National Geographic Traveler
Web site: http://www.nationalgeographic.com/traveler
Learn about exciting places all over the world with the stories and pictures in this magazine.

Travel Agent
One Park Avenue
New York, NY 10016
(212) 951-6600
Travel Agent has news and other information helpful to travel agents.

Travel Weekly
(800) 360-0015
e-mail: twcrossroads@cahners.com
Travel Weekly is a good magazine to read to learn all about the travel industry.

GLOSSARY

agency A company that helps people get work in a certain industry.

cabin A small living compartment in a ship, truck, or other vehicle.

cargo Goods transported in a ship, an airplane, a truck, a train, or another vehicle.

catapult A device for launching an airplane, usually from the deck of an aircraft carrier.

choreographer Someone who arranges and directs dances.

civilian A person not on active duty in the military.

commercial Something done in order to make a profit.

corporate travel agent A travel agent who works for specific companies rather than for the general public.

destination The end goal of a trip.

digital camera A camera that stores images on a disk instead of on film.

ecotourism Travel to areas of natural or ecological interest, usually with a guide, to learn about the environment.

freight Goods or cargo transported in a ship, an airplane, a truck, a train, or another vehicle.

integrity Honesty, dependability, and sincerity.

internship A job (sometimes unpaid) that allows you to get work experience in a particular field.

officiate To work as a referee or an umpire.

sonar A device for locating objects under water using sound waves.

survey To measure the size, shape, and position of an area of land, air, or water.

tip A wage given in addition to a worker's salary to show appreciation for the job done.

tripod A three-legged stand for a camera or another piece of equipment.

union (labor union) A group of workers who join together for better wages and working conditions.

yacht A small ship used for pleasure sailing or racing.

INDEX

About the Author

Simone Payment has a degree in psychology from Cornell University and a master's degree in elementary education from Wheelock College. She has taught elementary school, and worked in book publishing and for a health-care company. She is also the author of a biography of the Negro League baseball star Buck Leonard, a biography of the French explorer La Salle, and a book about Navy Seals.

Acknowledgments

The author would like to thank Heidi Friederich, Michelle Graziano, Tim James, John Riel, and Robin Shotola for their expert information and insights. She would also like to thank Jennifer Collins, Jason Jones, Mimi Linden, and Sarah Smith for putting her in touch with the experts.

Photo Credits

Cover © Brian Lawrence/Pictor; pp. 9, 10 © Frank Siteman/Index Stock Imagery, Inc.; p. 14 © Dan Gair Photographic/Index Stock Imagery, Inc.; pp. 19, 21 © Journalist 3rd Class Wes Eplen/U.S. Navy; p. 23 © Photographer's Mate Airman Alisha Clay/U.S. Navy; pp. 28, 29 © Jim Cummins/FPG International; p. 31 © Bettmann/Corbis; pp. 37, 39 © Neil Rabinowitz/Corbis; p. 42 © Barry Winiker/Index Stock

Design and Layout

Evelyn Horovicz